PLAYING

Written and illustrated by
Lesley Anne Ivory

Burke Books LONDON & TORONTO

First published April 1970
Reprinted May 1974

ISBN 0 222 99318 9 Hardbound
ISBN 0 222 66899 7 Limp
ISBN 0 222 99283 2 Library

Burke Publishing Company Limited,
14 John Street, London WC1N 2EJ.
Burke Publishing (Canada) Limited,
P.O. Box 48, Toronto-Dominion Centre,
Toronto 111, Ontario.
Printed in Great Britain by
T. & A. Constable Ltd., Edinburgh.

Sally likes to skip.

All children
like to play hide and seek.

Here's Tim driving his car.

Pat and James and David and Pam
go up and down on the see-saw.

"See how high you can jump,"
says Mary to John.

The boys fly their kites.

The girls play with their dolls.
Sara's doll has real hair.

It's fun to play marbles.

Sailing boats go fast in the wind.

"Oo-oo-oo!" call the Indians.

20

"'Let's ride to Banbury Cross,''
says Tony to Rosemary.